Nocturnal Animals

Raccoons

by J. Angelique Johnson

Consulting Editor: Gail Saunders-Smith, PhD

Consultant: Tanya Dewey, PhD
University of Michigan Museum of Zoology

CAPSTONE PRESS
a capstone imprint

Pebble Plus is published by Capstone Press,
151 Good Counsel Drive, P.O. Box 669, Mankato, Minnesota 56002.
www.capstonepub.com

 Books published by Capstone Press are manufactured with paper
containing at least 10 percent post-consumer waste.

Library of Congress Cataloging-in-Publication Data
Johnson, J. Angelique.
  Raccoons / by J. Angelique Johnson.
     p. cm. — (Pebble plus. Nocturnal animals.)
  Includes bibliographical references and index.
  Summary: "Simple text and full-color photos explain the habitat, life cycle, range, and behavior of raccoons"—
Provided by publisher.
  ISBN 978-1-4296-5288-9 (library binding)
  ISBN 978-1-4296-6194-2 (paperback)
  1. Raccoon—Juvenile literature. I. Title.
QL737.C26J644 2011
599.76'32—dc22   2010028745

Editorial Credits
Katy Kudela, editor; Ashlee Suker, designer; Marcie Spence, media researcher; Laura Manthe, production specialist

Photo Credits
123RF: Steve Byland, 7; Alamy: Rolf Nussbaumer Photography, cover; Crestock: Pdeleon, 11; Dreamstime:
Naturedisplay, 19; Fotolia: MacJac, 9; Minden Pictures: Dietmar Nill/Foto Natural, 21; Peter Arnold, Inc.: Delpho, M.,
13; Shutterstock: Frank Mathers, 1, Scott Rothstein, 5; Visuals Unlimited: Stephen Lang, 15, Steve Maslowski, 17

Note to Parents and Teachers

The Nocturnal Animals series supports national science standards related to life science.
This book describes and illustrates raccoons. The images support early readers in understanding
the text. The repetition of words and phrases helps early readers learn new words. This book
also introduces early readers to subject-specific vocabulary words, which are defined in the
Glossary section. Early readers may need assistance to read some words and to use the Table
of Contents, Glossary, Read More, Internet Sites, and Index sections of the book.

Printed in the United States of America in North Mankato, Minnesota.
072011
006231CGVMI

Table of Contents

Night Hunters

When the sun sets,

raccoons leave their dens.

These mostly nocturnal animals

come out after dark

for their nightly hunt.

There are three kinds of raccoons.

Raccoons live in North

and South America.

They make their dens in trees,

rocks, or on the ground.

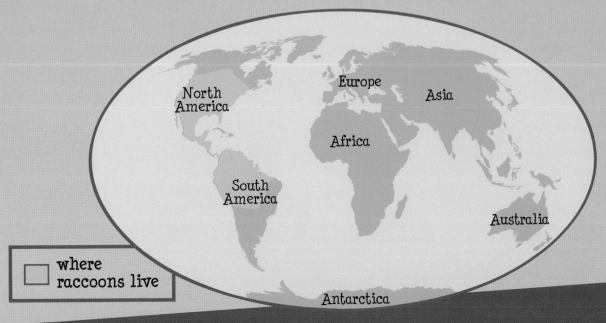

North
America

Europe

Asia

Africa

South
America

Australia

Antarctica

where
raccoons live

Up Close!

Raccoons have stocky bodies.
Most weigh between
8 and 22 pounds
(4 and 10 kilograms).

Raccoons blend in with the night.
Their ringed tails and dark fur
mix with shadows.
Their black masks make it
harder to see their eyes.

Raccoons have front paws
that look like hands.
They use their sharp claws
to climb, dig, and snatch prey.

Finding Food

Raccoons grab objects in the dark.

One sniff tells them if it's food.

Raccoons eat crayfish, frogs,

vegetables, and fruits.

They'll pick through garbage too.

Growing Up

In spring, females give birth

to up to seven kits.

Kits are born helpless.

To keep them safe, mothers

raise their kits inside dens.

At around 10 weeks, mothers teach their kits to hunt. Before they reach their first year, young raccoons leave the den to live by themselves.

Staying Safe

At night, raccoons watch
and listen for predators.

Scared raccoons show their teeth.

Raccoons that hide from danger
can live up to 16 years.

Glossary

crayfish—a small animal related to a lobster and crab that lives in fresh water

den—a small, protected space where a wild animal lives

kit—a young raccoon

nocturnal—happening at night; a nocturnal animal is active at night

predator—an animal that hunts other animals for food

prey—an animal that is hunted by another animal for food

stocky—short and heavy

Read More

Hurtig, Jennifer. *Raccoons*. Backyard Animals.
New York: Weigl Publishers, 2008.

Ripple, William John. *Raccoons*. Woodland Animals.
Mankato, Minn.: Capstone Press, 2006.

Internet Sites

FactHound offers a safe, fun way to find
Internet sites related to this book. All of the sites
on FactHound have been researched by our staff.

Here's all you do:

Visit *www.facthound.com*

Type in this code: 9781429652889

Check out projects, games and lots more at
www.capstonekids.com

Index

Word Count: 201

Grade: 1

Early-Intervention Level: 17